LET US GIVE THANKS

Meal and Gathering Prayers for All Occasions

AUTHORS
Gary J. Boelhower, Ph.D.
Daniele D. Flannery, Ph.D.
Patricia A. Lynch
John R. Schmitz, M.A.

HI-TIME Publishing Corp.

INTRODUCTION

It is an ancient and holy tradition that Christians pray together as they gather around the meal table. Eating reminds us of God's gift of life and the responsiblity we have to nourish each other with the bread of kindness and caring. Sharing food symbolizes the banquet of God's realm, in which all humankind will be one. Our meals call to mind Jesus' Last Supper with His friends as He shared His life in bread and wine.

This small booklet offers simple prayers expressing feelings that are a constant part of life—hope, need, sorrow, gratitude, forgiveness, joy.

The prayers may be used in many ways, for gatherings of all kinds. Those gathered for a celebration or meal may read a prayer together. Or one family or group member may read a prayer for all present. Any of the prayers may begin or end with the reading of the Scripture passage that is included with each prayer. Prayers may be combined to fit special situations, or they may be followed by a few quiet moments of reflection or by spontaneous prayers. And, of course, any of the prayers may be used for occasions other than the specific feast or occasion indicated.

However you use them, may these prayers help your family or group grow in love and appreciation of God and of each other.

Published with Ecclesiastical Permission.

Copyright © 1986, HI-TIME Publishing Corp.

Box 13337

Milwaukee, WI 53213

ISBN 0-937997-04-8

FOR SPECIAL OCCASIONS

1. Baptism
2. First Communion
3. Confirmation
4. Birthday
5. Wedding or Anniversary
6. Meal with Friends
7. Beginning of the School Year
8. End of the School Year
9. Graduation
10. Vacation

FOR SPECIAL FEASTS AND SEASONS

11. Feast of All Saints
12. Feast of Christ the King
13. Advent
14. Mary, Mother of God
15. Christmas
16. Feast of the Holy Family
17. New Year's Day
18. Lent
19. Easter
20. Pentecost
21. Winter
22. Spring

FOR SPECIAL NEEDS

FOR
SPECIAL OCCASIONS

1

BAPTISM

Loving God, we are grateful for this family celebration.

Baptism invites us to gather together

> to touch,
> to anoint,
> to mark with the sign of the cross,
> to put on white garments,
> to be renewed in words of faith,
> to pour the waters of promise,
> to give a new name.

Then Baptism challenges us

> to forgive when we are hurt,
> to hope when we're afraid,
> to share our gifts with those in need,
> to live in peace at home and afar,
> to act justly and uprightly with our brothers and
> sisters throughout the world.

God of life, give us the courage to live our Baptism daily.
> Amen.

1 Corinthians 12:4-7

FIRST COMMUNION

Lord Jesus, we rejoice that today
(name) has received you in the Eucharist
for the first time.
May *(name)* be filled with joy
and the strength of your presence.
And may all of us follow your example
by giving our lives for one another.
May we be like bread
broken and shared for each other.
May our love be poured out
like wine to refresh and bring joy.
Help us to live the Eucharist
by being openhearted in caring.
We ask this through Jesus,
who is our life today and every day. Amen.

John 6:47-51

3

CONFIRMATION

Spirit of change and growth, Spirit of rebirth and renewal, we rejoice in your presence and power. Nourished by your love and by the food and friendship of this family, *(name)* is taking an important step on the journey of faith. Thank you for the mystery of growth in *(name)* and in all of us. May this sacrament be a source of renewal for all of us, and may each Eucharist we share form us into a people of prayer and service.

This is a day of rejoicing. May our rejoicing last a lifetime and lead us to new and eternal life with you. Amen.

John 17:20-23

BIRTHDAY

God, our Creator, as we gather together
for this birthday celebration,
we are reminded that all life comes from you.
Today, we are especially grateful
for the life of *(name)*.
We thank you for another year of growth and sharing,
and we ask you to bless *(name)*
in the new year ahead.
Give to all of us your firm guidance
and your tender love.
This we ask in the name of Jesus
who celebrates with us here and
who promises to be with us forever. Amen.

Psalm 100

5

WEDDING OR ANNIVERSARY

Lord, you are a God of love and unending compassion.
As we rejoice in the union of love today, we ask
you to shower your abundant kindness on
(name) and *(name)*.

Keep them always close to each other and fill their
hearts with understanding and generous care.

May they always recognize that you are with them in
every joy and in every hardship.

May their love for each other continue to grow until
they are formed into that most perfect union
which we all await in your kingdom.

We pray for *(name)* and *(name)* in the name of Jesus,
who gives us the highest example of
self-sacrificing love forever. Amen.

1 John 4:7-8

MEAL WITH FRIENDS

We thank you, God, for gathering us
around this table to share
good food and friendship.
We praise you for the people
you have put on our pathway
to divide the burdens
and double the joys of our lives.
Help us always to support, encourage
and challenge one another.
May your gift of selfless love
bind us ever closer together
so that we may live as
brothers and sisters of your one family.
We pray in the name of the Father
and of the Son and of the Holy Spirit. Amen.

Philemon 1:4-7

7

BEGINNING OF THE SCHOOL YEAR

Time for school to begin again
    to see old friends, to meet new ones,
    to learn different things, from books, from
       teachers, from films and projects and field
       trips, from others in our school.

School is for people of all ages
    to learn about themselves and others,
    to learn how to make cabinets, to repair cars, to
       draw,
    to sing, and to work computers.

School isn't just for the people who go to classes.
    What is learned in school is to be shared with
    everyone.

As school begins again, we pray that students and
    teachers learn from each other, make good use of
    their talents, and share what they learn.

Micah 6:8

END OF THE SCHOOL YEAR

God, we wonder if you have noticed how different
things look at the end of the school year.

The teachers look a little tired and seem to have less
patience.

The erasers are all worn off our pencils.

Our notebooks and workbooks have ragged edges and a
worn-out look.

The classroom walls are filled with the projects we've
worked on all year long.

We tend to look out the window more — just dreaming
about a summertime of fun.

We feel a little smarter, even though we worked hard
and worried about passing some of those tests.

We feel thankful for our accomplishments and for your
goodness, God, in letting us learn about your
wonderful world. Amen.

Philippians 4:8-9

9

GRADUATION

Father, what a good feeling it is to graduate!
Graduation is one of those days that we often
think will never come.

All of those days we spent studying, reading, taking
exams, being called on in class — they're behind
us now.

But there are certain things we don't leave behind. We
have met some good people. We have learned
lessons of friendship and encouragement from
those we've come close to. We've learned how to
work and get along with others who are
different from us. Most of all we have
learned what it means to be part of a group —
to have people who care about us as we grow
and learn.

Thank you, God, for this happy day. The more we learn
about your world, the better we know you.

Sirach 51:13-17

VACATION

Loving God, vacation is one of your best creations!

It's good to sleep a little later, knowing we don't have
to be anywhere today. Yet we can plan to be
anywhere we want.

Vacation time gives us a chance to do something
different —
jump in the car and go for a drive,
visit faraway places,
spend the day on the beach,
stay home and read a book,
have lunch with a friend,
visit Grandma.

Most of all, we can enjoy our family being together. We
can discover again what a gift each member is
to us. We can laugh and sing and tell stories
and hug one another. We can thank you, God,
for giving us the time to be together. Amen.

Philippians 4:4-7

FOR
SPECIAL FEASTS
AND SEASONS

FEAST OF ALL SAINTS

Lord, we sometimes come to you hungry and tired, disappointed and sad. We know we cannot live on bread alone. We need your light and your love!

Today we rejoice with you, Lord, in all your holy people. They are reflections of your light and love. We thank you for the saints of the Church. *(Pause)* We thank you for friends and relatives who have shown us your compassion and care. *(Pause)* And we thank you for all the unknown saints in our world. *(Pause)*

As we share this meal, may we be renewed in hope and look forward to the day we will join you and your saints at your heavenly banquet. Amen.

2 Corinthians 4:5-7

FEAST OF CHRIST THE KING

When kings first began to rule,
    a king was a person who gathered the people
    together.
A king helped the people decide
    how they wanted to live together,
    what just rules they would have,
    how they would care for each other and
    act toward people outside their country.
Jesus was a king in this way, too.
Jesus gathered people together and taught them:
    Love as I have loved you.
    Forgive, feed and clothe, share and make peace
    with all. They are your neighbors.
Today, on the feast of Christ the King, we remember
    Jesus' words to us:
    Love as I have loved you.

Philippians 2:8-11

ADVENT

God of the universe,
God of our hearts,
we await your coming in joy.
May our time of Christmas preparation
make our hearts ready to receive you.
May we recognize you
in the cry of a baby,
in the care of a friend,
in the call for help of someone in need.
Open our eyes to the surprising ways
in which you come into our lives.
May our hands be prepared to give comfort and aid;
may our lips be ready to bless,
may our hearts be awake to your call.
We ask this in the name of Jesus,
who is coming today, even as we await
our Christmas joy. Amen.

Matthew 1:20-23

14

MARY, MOTHER OF GOD

Invite family or group members to pray the words which appear in bold print.

Dear God, we pray in thanksgiving.
For the gifted woman, Mary, whom you created,
    We thank you, God.
For the woman, Mary, who knew what it meant to make
    difficult decisions,
    We thank you, God.
For the woman, Mary, who gave life to Jesus,
    We thank you, God.
For the woman, Mary, who took time to visit her cousin,
    Elizabeth,
    We thank you, God.
For the woman, Mary, who, through her Son, brought joy
    to the wedding celebration at Cana,
    We thank you, God.
For the woman, Mary, who often pondered the meaning of
    Jesus in her life,
    We thank you, God.
For the woman, Mary, who stood faithfully by her Son at
    His tragic death,
    We thank you, God.
For the woman, Mary, who was filled with the gifts of the
    Spirit at Pentecost,
    We thank you, God.
For the woman, Mary, who challenges all of us to be
    faithful followers of Jesus,
    We thank you, God.

Luke 1:46-55

CHRISTMAS

Invite family or group members to pray the words which appear in bold print.

Christmas may be a time of special decorations or
      favorite foods,
        a time of spending time with people we care
        about,
        or a time of giving gifts.

Whatever we do to celebrate Christmas, let us
      remember that Christmas is really about giving
      love and receiving love.

Thank you, God, for people's love for us
shown through cards or presents or telephone calls or
cookies or hugs and kisses.
      Thank you, God.
Thank you, God, for our love for others
shown by listening or caring or making gifts for them.
      Thank you, God.
Thank you, God, for Christmas,
for a special time to give love
and a special time to receive love.
      Thank you, God.

Luke 2:1-7

16

FEAST OF THE HOLY FAMILY

Family is about

> belonging in a special way with people who share a
> history of being together for a time,
>
> belonging because of sharing every day together,
> of sharing fun things, sad and glad things,
> boring things and exciting things,
> of sharing food and toys, time and space, and
> attention.

It's not always easy being a family.

It's not always hard being a family.

But **it is** always work being a family.

> It's work to be many different people who are sharing
> life together.
> It takes effort to make beds, clean rooms, mow the
> lawn, forgive hurts, and say, "I'm sorry."

Trying to do all of this well is what makes our family holy.

Proverbs 24:3-4

NEW YEAR'S DAY

On New Year's Day we think of new beginnings.

>We'd like to be our best selves.
>We'd like the chance to change.

>*Invite each family member to consider one personal talent, gift or accomplishment of which he or she is proud and to share this pride if desired.*
>
>*Then invite each family member to consider a trait, habit, or characteristic that he or she would like to change and one way in which this can be changed. Family members may share thoughts on this if desired.*

Thank you, God, for this new year. Help us to enjoy every new day of it.

Thank you, God, for our best selves, for *(name of each person present).*

Help us to work at whatever change we have chosen and to support each other in our changing.

Isaiah 40:3-5

18

LENT

Lord, we are hungry
  for this meal, for your word, for love, for justice
  and dignity for all people, for peace in our
  world. *(Pause to add other concerns.)*
May this food we share lead us to think about those
who are hungry, poor and oppressed. May this food
lead us to be generous with our love and resources.

Be patient with us, Lord, as we make this Lenten
journey. Help us to keep from worrying about food and
drink and everyday cares. Help us to trust your mercy
and goodness. And help us to face our difficult days
with a sense of humor. Amen.

Isaiah 58:6-7

EASTER

Lord God,
we lift up our hearts in Easter joy
on this day of great celebration.
We rejoice in the resurrection of Jesus,
who has conquered death
and given us the promise
of everlasting life.
We are grateful for this food,
which sustains our bodies,
and for your Spirit of love,
which makes us one.
Help us to be a joy-filled people,
ready to share your happiness with others.
We ask this through Jesus Christ,
who is our risen Savior
today and always. Amen.

Matthew 28:8-10

20

PENTECOST

Invite family or group members to pray the lines which appear in bold print.

Jesus, this season reminds us of birth and growth. We see new life everywhere!

Lord, send us your Spirit.
Lord, send us your Spirit.

As we celebrate Pentecost, the birthday of the Church, we ask that you bless our Church, our parish, and all who lead us in prayer and service.

Lord, send us your Spirit.
Lord, send us your Spirit.

Renew us, Jesus, and help us to grow in your image. Form us into a community of persons who, like the apostles, are not afraid to speak your love, to live your love.

Lord, send us your Spirit.
Lord, send us your Spirit.

Bless this food we share, and help us to share the new life you give us through your Spirit. Amen.

Ephesians 3:14-17

WINTER

Lord, in this cold season, we draw close to one
another for warmth. But sometimes we are too close.
Impatient, short-tempered, restless, we need the understanding and compassion that come through your word
and your presence at this table.

    Help us respect one another's need for privacy and
       quiet.

    Help us forgive one another all the daily hurts.

    Help us be sensitive to the needs of our neighbors.

    And open us to the beauty and wonders of this
       season.

    Blessed are you, Lord, who provide us with food for
our table and joy for our hearts in all seasons. Amen.

Colossians 3:12-15

22

SPRING

Loving God, we're happy for this season.
It's like waking up —
    the covers of winter are thrown back.
There's a freshness, a hint of warmth in the air.
The light music isn't the radio, it's the sound of birds
    chirping.
The sun visits earlier now and leaves later. Its radiance
    embraces the earth.
The earth shakes its brown carpet until it turns green.
The trees graciously put on their Sunday best for
    nesting birds and longing admirers.

Spring is a time for coming to life again. Be with us,
    God,
    as we pause and pray for those places in our
    lives in which we want new life to spring forth.
    (Pause)

Psalm 147:7-11

SUMMER

Lord God, we thank you
for this season of summer.
The warm sunshine reminds us
of your constant care.
The beautiful flowers call us
to see your majesty and splendor.
Your earth is filled
with growth and goodness.
As we share the fruits of your creation,
help us to be a grateful people.
Open our hearts to recognize
all the gifts with which you bless us.
On these warm summer days,
help us to take the time
to rejoice in your loving presence.
We ask this in the name of Jesus,
who lives forever and ever. Amen.

Psalm 148:1-6

24

FALL

Lord, our lives are changing. The harvest is being gathered. The leaves are dying and the days are growing shorter. All creation is rushing to prepare for winter. We, too, are rushing, adding fall chores and celebrations to our long list of activities.

Slow us down, Lord, especially at this table. Help us to appreciate one another and to find the time to rejoice together in the beauty and mystery of this season. You are present in all the changes in our world and in our lives. Help us to see you and praise you in all things. Amen.

Psalm 67

VALENTINE'S DAY

God of love, today we show our love for you by showing
our love for one another.

So we send our hearts
to those who have given us life,
to those who have helped us grow and learn,
to those who have listened when we needed
someone,
to those we call our friends, especially our own
family.

When we send our hearts, we send all.

We promise that we're going to make today special.
But we also remember that we need to make
every day a heartfilled day, a day filled with
kind words and good deeds.

God, be with us now as we each name the people
special to us on this Valentine's Day. *(Invite all
to share the names of special persons.)*

1 Corinthians 13:4-7

FOURTH OF JULY

Dear God, this is some special day!
  We love the sights and sounds it brings,
    the happy sounds of marching feet and lively
    bands in parades,
    the friendly voices of families at playgrounds
    and picnics,
    the roar of fireworks lighting up the skies,
    the laughter of children splashing in pools.
  But most of all, we love the sound of the bell of
  freedom ringing in our ears,
    the freedom to love you as we wish,
    the freedom to learn and go to school,
    the freedom to work and build up your earth,
    the freedom to pursue peace and justice in our
    land and throughout the world.
Loving God of freedom, be with us as we pause for a
  moment of thanksgiving for the freedoms in our
  lives.

Psalm 100

MOTHER'S DAY

Today we remember our mothers and our grandmothers
and those women who came before them.

Mother's Day is for celebrating the special people in
our lives who have given us life in some way.

Today, God, we are grateful

for warm beds,
for a special treat,
for a nod which says, "I'm proud of you,"
for all the things which are done specially for us
and for which we often forget to say thank you.

And today we are especially grateful for *(names of
special people or special things they have done)*.

Luke 11:27-28

FATHER'S DAY

Dear God,
There are some things we'd like to say
about our dads as we celebrate Father's Day.
There are so many times we've forgotten to say
thank you, for all the good things that fathers do —
    for changing diapers and fixing cars;
    for teaching us to read
    and study the stars;
    for teaching us to laugh
    and teaching us to cry;
    for teaching us to play
    and reach for the sky.
    But most of all, for teaching us to love,
    a lesson they've learned from you, God, above.
So thank you, God, for the gift of our fathers. Amen.

Sirach 3:2-6, 12-14

THANKSGIVING

Lord, God,
we gather around this table
to express our thankfulness.
You give us everything that is good —
food for feasting,
family and friends to love us,
and a place of freedom on this earth.
We pray for the leaders of our country
and for all of us gathered here.
Help us to be peaceful
and grateful people.
We ask you this through Jesus,
who is the way to peace today and forever. Amen.

Philippians 4:4-7

FOR
SPECIAL NEEDS

PERSONAL THANKSGIVING

Father, our hearts are full! For personal achievement and success, for good news, for reunion and reconciliation, for all our blessings, we thank you and praise you. We thank you, too, for all the struggles and trials of life.

In calling us to be your people, you teach us that you alone are the source of life and goodness. May the food and conversation we share celebrate your goodness. May the blessings of this day become memories which nourish us in difficult times. And may we dedicate each day to thankfulness.

Father, thank you!

Luke 17:11-19

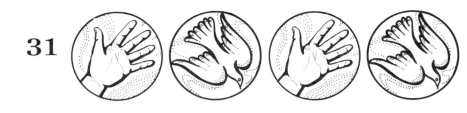

31

APPRECIATING SPECIAL GIFTS AND TALENTS

God,
you shower your abundant blessings upon us,
and we are grateful for all your gifts.
We thank you especially today
for *(talent or gift)*
which you have given to *(name)*.
May this special gift
remind us of your love for us.
May this talent and all of your blessings
be used to build up your community,
to make this earth a more joyful place
and your people a more loving family.
We ask this in the name of Jesus,
who lives with you in the unity
of the Holy Spirit, forever and ever. Amen.

1 Corinthians 12:4-7

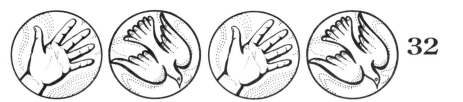

JOY

O God, every one of us has something to be joyful about,
something which gives us a warm feeling inside
     of surprise,
     of happiness,
     of being content with where we are at the moment.

Our joy can come from many things,

     watching the ocean as the tide changes,
     sitting and fishing by a quiet lake;

     seeing the first green leaves of spring,
     or the multicolored leaves of fall;

     sliding down a high water slide,
     having a good friend come to visit;

     eating our favorite food,
     running through the sprinkler on a hot summer day;

     remembering special times in the past,
     enjoying shelter during a thunderstorm.

     (Add some things which make you feel joyful.)

Help us take time to enjoy your gifts
     to know which things give each of us special joy,
     to stop and say, "How wonderful,"
     to clap our hands, to jump up and down, to dance, to
     run or to be still in our delight. Amen.

Philippians 4:4-7

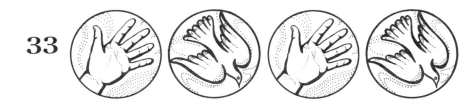

33

RECEIVING GOOD NEWS

Loving God, the shepherds received the good news of
Jesus' birth with joy. This news took away their fear
and sent them forth, telling others about Jesus.

We, too, love hearing good news

that comes in a letter from friends,
that comes with passing a test,
that comes when we learn that a faraway relative
is coming for a visit,
that comes when we are told a neighbor is recovering
after an operation,
that comes when we discover our cat just had kittens,
that comes when we receive a forgiving hug.

When we hear the Good News, God, we are hearing
that you love us. Filled with this love, we spread it
to others. Amen.

Luke 2:8-14

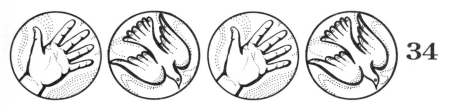

FORGIVENESS

Jesus, our brother,
we rejoice in your loving forgiveness.
You see our sinfulness,
the ways in which we hurt each other,
and, yet, you constantly call us back
to begin again.
You accept our faults and failings
and challenge us to a life
of tenderness, patience and faithful love.
Give us the courage to start anew,
to change our hearts,
and to follow your way.
We ask this through Jesus,
who is our way, our truth,
and our life, both now and forever. Amen.

Colossians 3:12-14

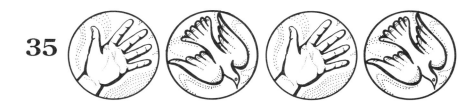

RECONCILIATION

Reconciliation means getting along with someone again.

You know, God, reconciliation isn't as easy as it sounds. Sometimes it means saying, "I'm sorry." It takes awhile to see you're wrong, and it takes even longer to tell someone that out loud.

Sometimes reconciliation means that two people were partly right and partly wrong. Then both people have to get over thinking they were completely right, and admit to each other that they were partly wrong.

To make matters worse, when there is some sort of disagreement or fight, things that hurt are said. That hurt sometimes stays on long past the words, "I'm sorry."

So, this reconciliation — this getting-along-with-people-again — takes a long time and a lot of work.

When we remember that you are forgiving of us, we can keep working to forgive others.

2 Corinthians 5:17-21

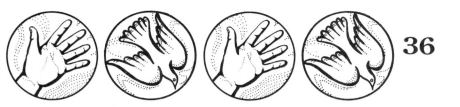

THINKING OF SOMEONE
WHO HAS DIED

God of Abraham and Sarah,
God of Isaac and Rebekah,
God of Jacob and Rachel,

you have called us to constantly remember those who have died, but still live on in our faith.

Today we want to remember those in our own family who have died.

We remember their smiling faces that told us they loved us.
We remember their warm touch that told us that they
  cared most of all.
We remember their thoughtful ways that made us feel so special.
We remember the stories they told that helped us know
  who they really were.
We remember how they loved to celebrate the fun things
  in life, even when times were tough.
We remember that they weren't perfect, but that they always did
  their best.
We remember how they lived their faith, so that it
  became our very own.

Today, we lovingly remember *(name)*. Amen.

Wisdom 3:1-9

IN TIME OF NEED

Father, you give us all good things. You know our every need and answer every prayer. You know that this is a difficult time for us. You know the silent prayers in our hearts. *(Pause)* In this and in all things, we pray that we may know and accept your will.

When our worries and hurts cause us to doubt, increase our faith and trust, and keep us mindful of your presence. Bless our conversation during this meal. May we support and encourage one another and help one another through this time of need. Amen.

Romans 8:26-27

IN SICKNESS

Invite family or group members to echo the first and last lines of this prayer, as indicated by bold print.

Lord, touch us with your healing and peace.
Lord, touch us with your healing and peace.
As we gather at this table, Lord, be merciful to us and extend your healing touch to your servant *(name)* who is sick. *(Pause)* Help us all to admit our need for you and to look beyond our aches and pains, our fears and worries.

We pray for all people who are sick. May they experience your compassion through those who care for them, and may they grow strong in your love.

Open our hearts, Lord, that we, too, may be ministers of your healing touch.

Lord, touch us with your healing and peace.
Lord, touch us with your healing and peace.

Psalm 25:4-7, 16-17

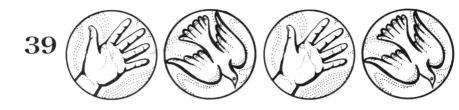

FACING A DECISION

We don't always understand what you have in store for us, Lord, but we know that you love us with an everlasting love. You hold us — our past, our present, our future — in your hands. For this we praise and thank you.

As we gather to share these gifts of food, we ask that you give us patience, insight and openness — gifts that will help us make a good decision. Help us take the time to pray. And help us hear your voice in the Scriptures and in the words of our family and friends. We trust you, Lord, today and always. Amen.

Matthew 18:19-20

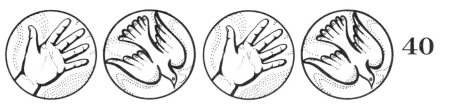

FOR THE POOR

Invite family or group members to echo the last line of this prayer, as indicated by bold print.

Lord, we give you thanks for this meal and for every meal that we share. And we thank you for the times when we are hungry. We may not know what it is like to be poor, but we try to see the world through your eyes. May this food and all the blessings of our home and family remind us of the needs of our brothers and sisters around the world.

Teach us, Lord, to share our bread and all that you have given us. May there always be room at our table and in our hearts for the unexpected guest. And may the day come when hunger and poverty are no more.

May your kingdom come!

May your kingdom come!

Luke 6:36-38